C000058030

Theosophy and
Esoteric Christianity

Also in this series:

Theosophy and the Search for Happiness
Texts by Moon Laramie and Annie Besant

Art and Theosophy
Texts by Martin Firrell and A.L. Pogosky

Forthcoming:

Theosophy and Clairvoyance
Texts by Kurt Leland and C.W. Leadbeater

Theosophy and Social Justice
*Texts by Dr. Barbara B. Hebert, William Quan Judge
& Annie Besant*

Theosophy and Yoga
Texts by Jenny Baker and Annie Besant

Theosophy & Esoteric Christianity

Texts by
Isis Resende,
R. Heber Newton
& Franz Hartmann

martin firrell company
MODERN THEOSOPHY

First published in 2019 by Martin Firrell Company Ltd
10 Queen Street Place, London EC4R 1AG, United Kingdom.

ISBN 978-1-912622-09-2

Design © Copyright Martin Firrell Company 2019.
Introduction © Copyright Moon Laramie 2019.
Essay © Copyright Isis Resende 2019.

All rights reserved. No part of this publication may be reproduced,
stored in or introduced into a retrieval system, or transmitted, in any
form, or by any means (electronic, mechanical, photocopying,
recording or otherwise) without the prior written consent of
the publisher.

This book is sold subject to the condition that it shall not, by way of
trade or otherwise, be lent, re-sold, hired out, or otherwise circulated
without the publisher's prior consent in any form of binding or cover
other than that in which it is published and without a similar condition
including this condition being imposed on the subsequent purchaser.

Text is set in Baskerville, 12pt on 18pt.

Baskerville is a serif typeface designed in 1754 by John Baskerville
(1706–1775) in Birmingham, England. Compared to earlier typeface
designs, Baskerville increased the contrast between thick and thin
strokes. Serifs were made sharper and more tapered, and the axis of
rounded letters was placed in a more vertical position. The curved
strokes were made more circular in shape, and the characters became
more regular.

Baskerville is categorised as a transitional typeface between classical
typefaces and high contrast modern faces. Of his own typeface, John
Baskerville wrote, 'Having been an early admirer of the beauty of
letters, I became insensibly desirous of contributing to the perfection
of them. I formed to myself ideas of greater accuracy than had yet
appeared, and had endeavoured to produce a set of types according to
what I conceived to be their true proportion.'

Introduction
by Moon Laramie

This volume of the *Modern Theosophy* series features essays on Christianity by the theosophists Isis Resende and Franz Hartmann and the Episcopalian clergyman R. Heber Newton. In her essay, *Theosophy and the Sacred Path of Christianity*, Isis Resende identifies 'a deeper level of Christianity that is not known among the general public.' Franz Hartmann argues that 'the Catholic Church, as a whole, may be regarded as an exoteric school of religion, and the different Orders therein as esoteric schools for practising Yoga.' For Hartmann, the aim of esoteric Christianity is not to 'seek to pry with one's intellect into the divine Mysteries, but wait in humility for their interior revelation.'

According to Isis Resende: 'There was the deliberate intention within the Catholic church of not letting the public have access to methods of spiritual transformation. This was achieved through the creation of a set of dogmas. This gave the church a lot of power over the population.' The second president of the Theosophical Society, Annie Besant, suggests that many began to turn away from Orthodox Christianity because of 'the crudity of the religious ideas set before them' and 'the gradual descent of Christian teaching into so-called simplicity'. Besant advocates that if Christianity is to reverse this decline, 'it must regain the knowledge it has lost, and again have its mystic and its occult teachings'.[1]

It is the practice of vicarious atonement in which others suffer and atone for our sins that Isis Resende maintains has 'impoverished Christian culture because it promoted the idea of saints and sinners with the church in between'. This orthodox practice removes from the average churchgoer 'his responsibility for his own life'. Theosophical author Geoffrey Farthing takes a similar view: 'It appears to many in the West, where we are concerned particularly with practical and not mystical or deep metaphysical thinking, that religious instruction is based on fundamental ignorance. We can, for example, make little or nothing of the doctrine of vicarious atonement.'[2]

It is only by direct and personal connection with the divine that the individual can spiritually evolve. In Franz Hartmann's opinion, the individual should realise 'the entire disappearance of the illusion of separateness; there is no separate self which knows, because the knower, the known and the knowledge are one.' It is in the eastern mystical tradition where this unity consciousness is most evolved. R. Heber Newton argues that for the majority of western Christians, God 'is an abstraction to them - a reality in which they themselves believe, but of whom they have no personal consciousness; with whom they feel themselves to stand in no actual relation... Now, the Eastern, whatever else he possesses, has the sense of God.'

Isis Resende points out that 'the Theosophical Society was in no small measure responsible for the spread of eastern philosophies and traditions in the West, particularly in the United States and Europe.' This spread of eastern traditions was begun by the Theosophical Society with the Parliament of the World's Religions, first held in Chicago and led by Annie Besant. R. Heber Newton comments that 'our famous American Theosophists, not content to stand with the seer in the gate, have gone out into the East, to find there the religion of the future.'

Christian scholars such as William Johnston and Thomas Merton have also travelled to the East and returned with new spiritual methodologies. Isis Resende cites Johnston's belief 'that we have to look for a Christian samadhi and this mysticism... must not be confined to the few who live inside the monasteries as has happened before.' R. Heber Newton identifies the importance of eastern doctrine, quoting the following passage from Ezekiel: 'He brought me to the gate, even the gate that looketh toward the East; and behold the glory of the God of Israel came from the way in the East.'[3] Newton adds that 'the wise, in a profounder ritual than that of men, face toward the East.'

Isis Resende suggests that ultimately, what eastern thought has to offer 'is the opposite of atonement... the idea of assuming responsibility for your life, your spiritual development, your happiness and the consequences of your actions.' She observes that 'looking at the sacred books is a process of asking and receiving, but asking from the heart'. Franz Hartmann believes that 'gradually ordered meditations and contemplations of the passion of Christ... may produce freedom from the illusion of self'. Perhaps R. Heber Newton best sums up the importance of a cross-fertilisation of eastern and western traditions. He contrasts the western Christian concept of man as separate from God and nature 'with that of the son of the East. His mind is sympathetic, constructive, intuitive; he sees the unity under all diversity; the whole in every part.'

1. Annie Besant, *Esoteric Christianity*, Theosophical Publishing Society, 1905

2. Geoffrey Farthing, *Theosophy, What's It All About?* Theosophical Publishing House, 1967

3. Ezekiel 43:1-2

Isis Resende

Isis Maria Borges de Resende is a lawyer who first joined the Theosophical Society on 1 August 1968. She later became president of the Alvorada Lodge in Brasilia, Brazil. She is a member of the board of directors of the Theosophical Society in Brazil and holds the post of Director of the Library of Theosophical Literature. Since 2014, she has been President of the Inter-American Theosophical Federation. Born into a family of theosophists, Isis remembers being interested in theosophical ideas from a very young age. Her father is a famous philanthropist and theosophist in America. Her grandmother has also made significant contributions to theosophy in Brazil.

Isis is an international speaker specialising in such subjects as meditation, the teachings of the Theosophical Society's founder H. P. Blavatsky, the Mahatma Letters, and Jungian ideas on dreams and symbols. She has lectured in Brazil, Argentina, Mexico, the USA, Portugal, Spain, Norway, Italy, the UK, India, Indonesia, New Zealand, Singapore and Russia.

With her husband, Rodrigo, Isis has delivered broadcasts for the Theosophical Society on television stations throughout Brazil. At one time, Isis and Rodrigo operated their own satellite TV station directly from their home. They broadcast a programming mix that was not only theosophical but also focused on related subjects including yoga, astrology and nutrition. Over the years they developed a substantial list of spirituality-based programmes in Portuguese, Spanish, and English.

In 2018, Isis visited the Theosophical Society in England to talk about the life and work of author Robin Amis. Amis lived and studied for several years in Mount Athos, Greece, making a significant contribution to modern Christianity in the West, drawing on ancient theological teachings preserved by the Greek Orthodox church. The text in this volume is based on that presentation.

Theosophy and the
Sacred Path of Christianity
Isis Resende (2019)

As a theosophist I am involved in the comparative study of the world's religions. This has awakened my interest in the sacred path in early Christianity. In this essay I will share my views on this subject and also its relationship to theosophy. To be clear, Tibetan Buddhism is my religion of choice but I am, for the most part, a practising theosophist.

One of the most important writers on the subject of Christianity's sacred path was an English author called Robin Amis. He was born in London in 1932 and died in 2014. I first came across his writing in 1998. I was hoping he would visit Brazil to talk about his work but there were some issues with permissions from his publisher and I was only able to speak to him by telephone.

Robin Amis was a very interesting figure. He was not a theosophist but, like many theosophists, he studied different religions. He explored Hinduism and Kabbalah as well as the teachings of Gurdjieff and Ouspensky. So he had a general grasp of a range of spiritual teachings and he was able to profit from his studies with the Eastern Orthodox church. This enabled him to bring a new vision of Christianity to the West and I found his vision particularly interesting. One of his most famous books is entitled, *A Different Christianity*. In this work, Amis describes a deeper level of Christianity, unknown to the general public.

There was a particular moment in history - a crossroads - that still has great influence and great relevance for us today. The Roman Empire became Christian in the 4th Century AD. At the time, the empire was already in decline. The emperor Constantine established the city of Constantinople in the east, known today as Istanbul, and made it the new capital of the Roman Empire.

Several years later the Roman Empire in the west, with its capital in Rome, broke down completely. The Roman Empire in the east fell to the Turks eleven centuries later. These events created a schism in the Christian church. There was the Roman Catholic church ruled over by the popes in the Vatican and this had a tremendous influence on western society in the Middle Ages. The Roman Empire in the east gave rise to the Orthodox churches which were divided up more or less between different countries, much as the different national sections of the Theosophical Society are today. So there are the Orthodox churches of Greece, Syria, Russia, Bulgaria and so on. The Orthodox churches had patriarchs who perform a similar role to the popes in the Roman Catholic church.

Although they were all Christians, reading from the same literature, as time passed, their ideas began to develop in different directions. For example, the Orthodox churches knew nothing of Frances of Assisi, Teresa of Avila or John of the Cross, and the Roman Catholic church knew nothing of Anthony the Great or St. Theophan the Recluse. For centuries they progressed along separate paths in their respective regions.

During the 18th and 19th Centuries, and particularly in the 20th Century, immigration increased dramatically. Therefore some of the teachings that were known only in the Orthodox churches began to be brought to the West and vice versa. This exchange of ideas was what led Robin Amis to go to Mount Athos.

Mount Athos could be said to be the Vatican of the Orthodox church in Greece. Amis stayed there for more than twelve years, studying and interacting with the monks and probably learning Greek as well.

There is another idea that has had a powerful influence on our lives today and on the new Christian literature currently being published: throughout history, there has always been an esoteric aspect to Christianity. This hidden doctrine was known only inside the monasteries, and to some mystics and intellectuals. It was never revealed to the general public. There was the deliberate intention within the Catholic church to deny the public access to certain methods of spiritual transformation and this was achieved through the creation of dogmas.

These dogmas gave the church a great deal of power over the population. For example, one of them is the dogma of atonement. Here a person needed a priest if he was to be saved. He could not go to God directly. This impoverished Christian culture because it promoted the simplistic and polarised idea that you were either a saint or a sinner with the church in between as ultimate mediator. Therefore a person could take no direct action for his own salvation.

It was the priest who would save someone, not that individual's own efforts, not his own virtues. If somebody was a terrible sinner but repented to his priest at the last moment then he would go to heaven. That was it. This dogma of atonement had a very negative influence on society, taking from a Christian his responsibility for his own spiritual life. What Robin Amis talks about in *A Different Christianity* is the exact opposite of atonement. He talks about self-experience. He explores the idea of assuming responsibility for your life, your spiritual development, your happiness and the consequences of your actions.

It is important to note that the Theosophical Society was in no small measure responsible for the spread of eastern philosophies and traditions in the West, particularly in the United States and Europe. Although these traditions also had an esoteric side, they were less influenced by politics.

Buddhism, in common with other similar belief systems, was more open about the methods one should practise for self-development. Meditation is one such method that is given particular emphasis in eastern culture.

The spread of eastern traditions in the West was started by the Theosophical Society in 1893 with the Parliament of the World's Religions, held in Chicago and led by the Theosophical Society's second president, Annie Besant. It was here that the western world gained true insight into Hinduism and Buddhism. Previously those faiths had been considered nothing more than superstitions and cultural fantasies. After 1893, the eastern methodologies were better and better known in the West and this posed a threat to the various Christian traditions.

Up until this point, the Church had shared some very simplified teachings - if you are good and go to church, you go to heaven. The eastern religions had a more didactic way of presenting their beliefs. They encouraged people to practise techniques for their own self-development. As a result, the intelligentsia began to look increasingly to the East for spiritual answers rather than to the West. Because of this threat, the Christian authorities began to reveal some of the rare pearls of spiritual wisdom that had been hidden inside the monasteries for centuries.

The experience on Mount Athos described in *A Different Christianity* is just such a pearl, presented by Robin Amis for the benefit of western readers. Using Christian terminology, Amis reveals ideas that are even easier to recognise in the literature of the eastern traditions.

He tells us that there is no need to turn to eastern philosophy and literature. Everything can be found in western Christianity. This is in many ways an admission of the threat now facing the established traditions of the Christian church. Not just the work of Robin Amis, but also the work of Jacob Needleman, John Main, Thomas Merton, William Johnston all give similar expression to this crisis.

William Johnston and Thomas Merton travelled to the East and studied there for a long time. They became familiar with Theravada Buddhism and Zen. They brought back Theravada Buddhism and Zen methods to the West but with Christian terminology. Christian culture is being enriched by contact with the Orthodox churches as well as by Christians who have written about their spiritual experiences in the Far East.

John Main was an Englishman who travelled to Thailand and had powerful experiences of Transcendental Meditation. When he returned to England, he looked for something similar within Christianity. He wanted Christians to be able to practise what he had practised in Thailand. He wrote books on what he called Christian meditation and these have been used in several monasteries in Canada, the United States and Europe. Twenty years ago, the word 'maranatha' was unknown. It was brought to the West by John Main. Today it is a mantra used in Christian monasteries and an example of the ongoing influence of the eastern traditions on modern Christianity.

William Johnston spent ten years in Japan. In his book, *Zen Christianity*, he suggests that we have to look for a Christian 'samadhi', or enlightenment, and that this mysticism, this practice, must be shared with the public. It must not be confined to the few who live inside the monasteries as has happened before. This is a good time for Christianity. Ground-breaking literature is being released describing a Christianity that has always existed but was not accessible to everyone. One interesting thing about

Robin Amis' experiences on Mount Athos is that he studied under a monk who told him: 'You English have helped the world move forward, providing solutions to many problems that have made life easier for many. Now it is time for you to do different work - to understand and tell the world the inner truth, the truth of the heart.' What he was really saying was that Robin Amis should study deeply and reveal to the world the sacred path of Christianity.

The word 'path' is used a great deal in eastern literature. Some people call it discipleship. H.P. Blavatsky uses the words 'the path of the heart' and 'the secret path'. Here the use of the word is similar. Particularly in *The Voice of the Silence*, she uses the terms 'the secret path', 'the secret way'. Here she is describing a way of developing yourself more quickly to benefit the world - you cannot benefit others without first benefitting yourself. You cannot give what you don't have, so the relationship between benefitting others and benefitting yourself is absolute. This is called the path of the heart.

In *A Different Christianity*, Robin Amis writes, 'Christianity has possessed and still possesses an inner tradition. This is not a system but a discipline.

But for several reasons, among them the need to confine itself to a scientific view, it has been losing the power to illuminate and transform people.' He suggests a solution to this loss of power, saying, 'To understand the possibility that Christianity offers, we need new eyes and yet a very old way of thinking about the world.'

Theosophy talks about the ancient wisdom, this very old way of thinking. This concept is also found in the name theosophy, formed from the words 'theos' and 'sophia'. 'Theos' is the divine and 'sophia' is wisdom. This wisdom of the divine is, itself, a very old way of thinking.

Amis goes on to say that we can draw on texts like the Bible to deal with all our daily problems. This is the exact opposite of atonement. For atonement you need a priest to lead you to God but here you use only the Bible. You can take nourishment from its texts that relate to your own experience. It gives you a fresh perspective. The Bible should not be taken as a historical text.

This is also true of the Dhammapada, the Bhagavad Gita and the Qur'an. It is true of all sacred texts. We can take from them what we need for our day-to-day experience. This is most definitely a different kind of Christianity.

When Roman society became too politicised, Robin Amis explains that the true mystics went into the desert and founded the first monasteries far away from the conflicts in society. This 'royal route' or 'secret route' is a cure for the soul. We must cure our inner selves using the texts of the sacred books. Amis suggests that reuniting our thinking faculties with the heart is the great secret. He argues that it is not an occult or hidden truth but something that simply tends to go unnoticed because of our lack of understanding. We change our minds more easily than we change our feelings. All our inconsistencies exist because our thoughts and our feelings are moving in opposite directions. For example, in theosophy, we can understand the concept of universal brotherhood but still have a strong dislike for somebody. We accept the concept in our heads but not in our hearts. Uniting our thought processes and our hearts is extremely important. But how can we do that? By a process of assimilation. You can eat a piece of bread but how long does it take for its nutrients to get into your bloodstream? It has to go through a whole process of digestion: the separation of the nutrients from the waste that will be expelled. The process of assimilation is more important than the process of eating itself.

In theosophy there is a correlation between our time in each incarnation on earth and our time spent in Devachan. When we are living in a human body and having different experiences it is as if we are 'eating'. When we are in the after death states it is as if we are assimilating what we have eaten into our spiritual bloodstream. In the next incarnation, we are not the same as when we died because we have assimilated all of the ideas from our previous life. The process of assimilation is very important and meditation plays an essential role. Just reading a book is very different from meditating on that book. When you meditate on what you have read, you go deeper into the text and it becomes part of your being. Your heart responds to it. When the teachings from the book stay only in your mind, then your actions, feelings and ideas may not be in alignment.

It is important to align the thinking faculty with the heart. We must feel with the brain as well as with the heart and that requires a process of self-knowledge.

Robin Amis makes repeated reference to the Bible text in Matthew 7:7:8 which says, 'Ask and you will receive. Search and you will find. Knock and the door will be opened. Because everyone that asks receives. Everyone that seeks finds. For everyone that knocks, the door is opened.' But we don't always see the profound truth of this text and Amis identifies the problem here as a lack of purity in the heart. We do not ask sincerely. We don't ask often enough or we evade the issue. We need to create the conditions for asking and receiving.

Mark 2:17 tells us that Jesus said, 'The ones that are whole need no physician,' and he came in order that the sinners should repent. This word 'repentance' is a poor translation of the Greek word 'metanoia'. Metanoia is about repentance but it is not just that. When you repent, you feel regret about something you did. But metanoia means changing your mind, changing the state of your consciousness. 'Meta' means 'beyond'. 'Noia' means 'concrete mind' and metanoia means 'beyond the concrete mind'. That suggests a spiritual perception.

For this spiritual perception to be realised we have to put aside certain things that prevent it from manifesting itself. Amis emphasises that the saints were not born holy. They became holy. So there is a process of self-transformation, a process of becoming more and more able to manifest that spiritual energy that is available to us.

No one can create spirituality. Our spirituality is within us but we have to deal with what prevents that spirituality from manifesting. In his very Christian way, Robin Amis says, 'Pray for help.' He says that the 'royal road' or the 'secret path' is based on the psychology of prayer. This prayer is not simply a mental exercise but should be practised to transcend the mind's limitations with the help of prayer's essential energy. People say you cannot change things on your own, you should ask for help. We might doubt this but the most popular way of meditating in Christianity is through prayer. You can use prayer to bargain with God. You can say to God, 'If I give You this, then You give me that.' But there are other ways of praying. The simplest way is by giving thanks. You can give thanks for all kinds of things: for who you are, what you have, the opportunities you are given. If you say to God, 'I pray and You must give me this', then what and where is God? Is it a He or a She up in the clouds? Is there a person called God? God is the unity of life, the essence of everything. How can you ask the essence of everything to give you something? But if you focus your mind on the higher planes, then you connect with those higher levels inside yourself, because they are always there. For this reason, prayer can be very useful.

We can also change the way we think. Each of us has a different personality. Our consciousness seems somehow limited to our environment. But that is simply the condition we have been born into. We have lived previous lives with different experiences. When we look within, we may resurrect dormant capacities we didn't know we had because we acquired them in another life. They were gained under other circumstances. Therefore going higher or going deeper is the same thing. There is no 'on high' or 'up there'. In actuality, it is elevating one's mind to a more subtle condition. This idea of going deeper is symbolised by praying to God. We might pray to Francis of Assisi or

Master Jesus, but will he be able to answer everybody's prayers? Will he be answering our 'spiritual emails'? Doesn't he have more important work to do?

In his book, *Self Realization Through Love*, I. K. Taimni tells us that when we have this attitude of devotion and of prayer, we touch the inner side of life. This is where we can find our answers, not from this person or that person. This is what is meant by the words 'pray for help'. We have to transcend our current state of mind by the process called metanoia and this is symbolised by the well-known parable of the prodigal son.

The younger of two sons asks his father to give him his share of the estate. The boy cannot wait for his father's death for his inheritance. He wants it straightaway. The father agrees and divides his estate between both his sons. On receiving his portion of the inheritance, the younger son travels to a distant country and wastes all his money in extravagant living. Soon a famine strikes the land. He becomes desperately poor and is forced to take work as a swineherd. When he finds himself envying the pigs' food, he comes to his senses at last.

He says, 'How many hired servants of my father's have bread enough to spare, and I'm dying with hunger! I will get up and go to my father, and I will tell him, *Father, I have sinned against heaven, and in your sight. I am no more worthy to be called your son. Make me as one of your hired servants.*' He set off towards his father's house. But while he was still far off, his father saw him and, moved with compassion, ran towards him, falling on his neck and kissing him. The son does not even have time to finish his rehearsed speech, since the father calls for his servants to dress him in a fine robe, a ring, and sandals, and slaughter the 'fattened calf' for a celebratory meal.

The older son, who was at work in the fields, hears the sound of celebration, and is told about the return of his younger brother. He says to his father, 'For many years I have served you, and I have never disobeyed an order, but you never gave me a goat, so that I could celebrate with my friends. Yet when my brother came home, having squandered your money on prostitutes, you killed the fattened calf for him.' The parable concludes with the father explaining that because the younger son had returned, in a sense, from the dead, celebration was necessary: 'But it was appropriate to celebrate and be glad because your brother was thought to be dead and is alive again. He was lost and now he is found.'

In the parable, the prodigal son finds his way back to his spiritual home where he had everything. So in a way we are all prodigal sons and daughters, living more or less miserable lives and somehow longing to reunite with our spiritual nature, which is our real home. But that is only possible if we remove the obstacles in our path - our wrongdoings, our mistakes and misunderstandings. This is how Robin Amis puts it. Metanoia will not come easily, but only after a struggle and only once our change of heart becomes permanent. First there is a fall. Our lives are full of wrongdoing. Then we receive the results of that wrongdoing as karma returns that energy to us. When this happens, we awaken and our awakening leads us to make new decisions. Once we take that new path, this results in a new attitude and a new way of life.

Of course it's a simplified way of saying that we must accept the consequences of our actions and change our ways through metanoia. This metanoia is a process composed of two different attitudes. One is called diacrisis, a Greek word which means observation, attention, a process of realising what is preventing you from really leading a happy spiritual life. What are the things that are weighing you down? This can also be described as a process of purification because if we are too heavy then the spiritual energies, that are more subtle, are not perceived. There is a movement from beneath upwards. That is the movement of diacrisis. But there is another form of movement. That movement is grace. This is the energy we receive when we remove the obstacles on our path. These two things together - purification from beneath and the blessing that comes from above - make our spiritual transformation possible. And that is metanoia. By praying, remembering all the time that there is a spiritual dimension within us, by making the proper efforts to remove what prevents grace from manifesting, we are on the royal road of Christianity, on the sacred path of Christianity.

Amis says, 'The sacred path is a way of turning grace into permanent experience.' Our wrongdoings are very powerful so in order to overcome them we need to activate an even mightier power. This is demonstrated in the parable of the ten virgins in Matthew 25:1-13.

'Then the Kingdom of Heaven will be like the ten virgins who took their lamps and went out to meet the bridegroom. Five of them were foolish and five were wise. Those who were foolish took no extra lamp oil with them. Those who were wise took spare oil in vessels with their lamps. Now while the bridegroom was delayed, they all slept. At midnight there was a cry, 'Look! The bridegroom is coming! Come out to meet him!' Then all the virgins arose and trimmed their lamps. The foolish said to the wise, 'Give us some of your oil because our lamps are going out.' But the wise said, 'What if there isn't enough for us and for you? It's better if you go and buy more lamp oil for yourselves.' While they were gone buying oil, the bridegroom came, and those who were ready went in with him to the marriage feast, and the door was shut. Afterwards the other virgins also came, saying, 'Lord, Lord, open to us.' But he answered, 'Most certainly I tell you, I don't know you.' Watch therefore, for you don't know the day nor the hour in which the Son of Man is coming.'

There is an esoteric interpretation of this parable. The five virgins are the five senses. If they are aware, lit by the fuel of gladness, of happiness, of grace, when the moment comes they will be taken on the spiritual path. But if they go to sleep, if they don't have this fuel of grace, gladness and happiness, when the moment comes, they are not prepared and cannot start out on the spiritual path.

We can each choose wisely how we use our senses. Are we going to acquire the fuel of gladness, of happiness, of grace, preparing ourselves with attention and observation, removing all the obstacles that prevent us from being really spiritual. Are we going to allow grace to flow or are we going to go to sleep? It's a choice for every one of us. All of us are responsible for our own gladness or our own misery. And depending on what we think, what we feel, how we act, we receive the karmic consequences. No saint is born a saint. We must each work for it. We must make an effort from below, aspiring upwards, and allow this grace to flow.

There are some words spoken by the living Jesus. Not the one that died two thousand years ago but the Christ within ourselves:

And he said, 'Whoever finds the interpretation of these sayings will not experience death.'

Jesus said, 'Let him who seeks continue seeking until he finds. When he finds, he will become troubled. When he becomes troubled, he will be astonished, and he will rule over the All.'

Jesus said, 'If those who lead you say to you, 'See, the kingdom is in the sky,' then the birds of the sky will precede you. If they say to you, 'It is in the sea,' then the fish will precede you. Rather, the kingdom is inside of you, and it is outside of you. When you come to know yourselves, then you will become known, and you will realise that it is you who are the sons of the living father. But if you will not know yourselves, you dwell in poverty and it is you who are that poverty.'

So what do we choose for ourselves? Poverty? Or do we choose to follow this secret path that will lead us to the spiritual heights, to a life of blessings and happiness, a life in which we are really able to help others. It's a choice for every single one of us.

R. Heber Newton

Richard Heber Newton (31 October 1840 - 19 December 1914) was a prominent American Episcopalian priest and writer.

Newton was rector of All Souls' Protestant Episcopal Church in New York City from 1869 to 1902 and he was an important leader in the Social Gospel movement. This branch of Protestantism, set out to apply Christian ethics to social problems, especially issues of social justice including economic inequality, poverty, alcoholism, crime, racial tensions, slums, poor sanitation, child labour, inadequate labour unions, inadequate schools, and the danger of war.

Newton was a committed supporter of historical criticism of the Bible and aimed to unify Christian churches in the United States. His 1874 - 1875 lectures, *The Morals of Trade*, were seen as an important early statement expressing many of the concerns which were prominent in the Social Gospel movement.

In 1883, he was accused of heresy for a series of sermons later published in a book, *The Right and Wrong Uses of the Bible*. He was again accused of heresy in 1884 and 1891.

In 1903, he served as first and last pastor of Stanford Memorial Church at Stanford University.

His publications include *Studies of Jesus* (1880), *Womanhood: Lectures on a Woman's Work in the World* (1881) and *The Mysticism of Music* (1915).

The Influence of
the East on Religion
R. Heber Newton (1913)

The 'gate that looketh toward the East', of which Ezekiel wrote, has been to many others than the prophet the observatory whence is seen the oncoming glory of the Eternal. A very old and very widespread instinct is that which leads man, on entering his chamber for communion with God, to throw open the window whose prospect is toward the East. Orientation has a deeper meaning than our ecclesiastics fancy. The noblest form of Nature-worship was that of which we may find traces on many a hill of England, where our fathers gathered in the dawn of day to hail with sacred song the coming of the Sun. As needs must be in a cosmos - a beautiful order, the core and centre of whose physical system is a moral order - the cosmical truth enshrines an ethical truth, and the symbolism of Nature becomes a sacrament of Spirit. Of the Light which is 'on-coming into the world', as St. John says, it is true that 'His goings forth are as the morning' - the pathway of Divine progress in humanity, an ascension of the Sun of Righteousness toward the zenith. The history of man repeats the story of the natural order, and 'Westward the star of Empire takes its way'; civilisation and religion arising in the

East, and moving thence in successive effluences toward the West. Whither the Spirit of the Eternal led the soul of Ezekiel, thither the same Divine Spirit has led other human souls in different lands and at different critical epochs, to watch for signs of fresh light; and they who have come down to their fellows with the glow of a new day on their faces have, whether in Babylon, or Rome, or London, told the same story: 'He brought me to the gate, even the gate that looketh toward the East; and behold the glory of the God of Israel came from the way in the East.

Once more, if men cry to the Watchers: 'Watchmen, what of the night?' the answer floats down: 'The morning cometh'; and the wise, in a profounder ritual than that of men, face toward the East.

That a new flood of spiritual life must be soon due, he feels sure who has marked well the movements of the tides of history and guessed the cycles of the stars. The ebbing of the tide of materialistic speculation is felt beneath the feet of them that reason well; and the sucking undertow of the social waters, in a new wave of ethical enthusiasm, a fresh force of justice and brotherliness, is heard by those whose ears are close to the sands of the shore. Whence is the new tide coming on whose floods we are to float across the shallows of the age? In every direction we see in society the evils of an excessive development of the tendencies which are peculiar to our Western civilisation. The elements which form our strength in the realms of thought, of feeling, and of action, have been pushed beyond the golden mean; and the result is, as in all disproportion, error and evil. If our human therapeutics at all shadow the divine dealings, we might expect the correction of these disorders by the supply of the elements lacking in our own blood. The qualities which the western world lacks, the Eastern world holds in excess. We might then look for the ordering by Providence of an infusion of the essence of the East; the balm of Gilead for the wounds of England, the cordial of India for the tire of America.

Singular, indeed, to him who believes in no Destiny that shapes our ends, is the re-discovery of the East by our century; the bringing of its mystic lands from out the darkness; the establishing of close connections between the two hemispheres; the unsealing of the sacred books of the East for the study of the West.

Some years ago, when, being younger, I thought in my folly that I held a private patent of expectation, I heard one of our wisest teachers of religion in this city give me back my own dream, saying to me: 'I look for a new religious impulse from the East.' And then it seemed that everyone who thought was saying with Tyndall: 'Light will come again from the East.' We find ourselves, as by common instinct, standing in 'the gate that looketh toward the East,' where rise, on our impatient eyes the streakings of a new and holy light, and we whisper: 'Behold the glory of the God of Israel cometh from the way of the East.'

Some over-hasty souls, like our famous American Theosophists, not content to stand with the seer in the gate, have gone out into the East, to find there the religion of the future. They are finding, I fancy, that which a friend told me he had found for himself; when, driven away from traditional Christianity, he had in the old world mastered the Pāli tongue, that he might search among the sources of Buddhism for the higher light, only to come home again with the conclusion that, at least, there was nothing there higher than the truth which is found in Christianity. What we may reasonably expect is not the coming of a new religion from the East to supersede Christianity, but the coming of the influences from the East to renew and restore Christianity. Our lamps burn low, but we need not cast them away; we should simply open them to the sacred oil from the East, which the High Priest of the Temple is even now pouring in upon the wicks - when, lo! a new flame in which we shall see and rejoice. Those who heard the dark-skinned Hindu Mozoomdar speak and pray in our churches, or who have more lately heard Swami Vivekananda or Swami Abhedananda lecture must feel, as in no other way they could have felt, that if our Western faith had aught to give them and their countrymen, as we all believe, they have somewhat to give us in return.

I

The Eastern's thought of Nature may greatly help us of the West. Do we think, in our egotism, that we have for the first time in the history of man studied Nature? We may draw a just rebuke from our rapidly increasing knowledge of those wise men who, in Egypt, and Chaldea, and India, observed and pondered, and laid the foundations of the noblest of our physical knowledges. If we fancy that we alone of the children of earth have divined the secret order of creation, we may learn humility as we acquaint ourselves with the wonderful divination by which they anticipated the greatest of our later guesses. And so coming to appreciate the patient brooding thought over the problem of the cosmic, the slow, sure following of the trail of Nature on the part of these dark-skinned sages, we shall be prepared to allow, more modestly, that there may be something in their view of Nature which we may need, as we know that there is much in our view of Nature which they need. Our Western mind is analytic, logical; breaks up Nature into bits; conquers in the sign of the test tube and the crucible; deals with phenomena; pursues the sequences of physical processes; familiarises itself with the action of forces and the methods of laws; and, in so doing, does wisely and wins our wonderfully widening knowledge. But our very development of power is, as always, in the parsimony of Mother Nature, at the cost of other powers. Contrast our study of Nature with that of the son of the East. His mind is sympathetic, constructive, intuitive; he sees the unity under all diversity; the whole in every part. He is fascinated by the conception of the substance, the reality, lying under all phenomena. He passes without interest through the surface-fields of law and force, and faces this eternal mystery of being, on which all phenomena of existence play, as the bubbles thrown up for a moment upon the surface of the everlasting stream. We call him an idealist, a dreamer. He calls us sense-blinded materialists. His limitations are plain to us, and our limitations are as plain to him. Each sees through one eye. Man needs both eyes focusing on Nature to get the true light. We may learn to credit his vision as revealing an essential part of truth, as we find his vision to be that of the profoundest thinkers of our Western world, from Plato down to Hegel. We will never probably turn away from our scientific vision. That is true, as far as it goes. But we may open the other eye and correct its one-sidedness, and see that which it alone failed to reveal. Then all our present miserable notion of a conflict of science and religion will vanish like a ghost of the night. It will be seen to be a spectre of the twilight. The East knew of our theory of Evolution centuries before Spencer established it scientifically, or Darwin applied it to man's story, or Huxley bore down with it so aggressively on faith. It was the cardinal doctrine of the sages of India. But those calm minds, sitting beneath the palm trees by the sacred rivers, thought through the problem in the outer meshes of which our hastier minds are too easily detained. Their vision of Evolution only deepened the mystery of the universe. The fact of an orderly and gradual development of life, through the stages of creation, held nothing of the secret of life itself. Such a process could be only the manner of the unfolding of the 'somewhat' charged with all these marvellous potencies. That 'somewhat' - the substance or reality standing under all phenomena - was the Infinite Mystery, to know which was to know the secret of being. No investigation of the materialist could discover the secret of being which gave substance to our mental forms in their subtle phantasmagoria. Mind alone, which pondered over this mystery, could image its being. It was mind, intelligence.

Out of thought's interior sphere
These wonders rose in upper air.

Confirmed idealist as was the Hindu philosopher (I speak of the dominant school of philosophy, that which permanently characterised India), he could speak of the material world only in terms of mind. Evolution became the doctrine of the progressive unfolding of life through the action of an Infinite and Eternal Spirit. It was, it is, the history of the Divine Being. It was, it is, a religion. And this Eastern wisdom our Western world cannot reject as an alien conception when not alone idealist philosophers like Berkeley hold it, but savants like Huxley confess that, as between the two conceptions of idealism and materialism, they would have to take the first theory. True, they talk of a possible third conception, the conciliation of both; of which it will be time to speak when the shadow of any such thought looms above the horizon.

Our Western world, gone daft over the fascinating theory of evolution, and fancying that in it is solved the problem of being, in terms of matter, may turn to the sages who had divined our pet theory centuries ago, and to whom it had become a translucent symbol of the Divine Presence and action. Our own poets who drink of the Castalian springs of Western philosophy are those who, like Emerson, are interpreting for us the real significance of our scientific theories and showing us how to worship where we only thought to study. Standing in the gate that looketh to the East, these seers behold the glory of the Lord coming upon our wisdom of Nature by the way of the East gate.

II

This insistent idealism in philosophy, which the East may have again to teach the world, lays the basis for religion, deep, and broad, and firm. Resting upon this basis, the Eastern mind, through its peculiar spiritual sense, opens the world in which the soul of man communes with God. The Oriental seems to have developed a sense which is lacking in most of us children of the West. One sees about him in our society hosts of men, excellent, admirable, noble, upright and conscientious, faithful in every relation of life, who appear to have no sense by which to apprehend God. He is an abstraction to them - a reality in which they themselves believe, but of whom they have no personal consciousness; with whom they feel themselves to stand in no actual relation. The story of spiritual experiences comes to them in an unknown tongue. Their conclusion concerning such matters is fairly expressed in the common account they give of those who speak of such experiences - 'You are peculiarly constituted; you are spiritually organised.' Now, the Eastern, whatever else he possesses, has the sense of God. Religion's home is in the East. Its power there is almost tyrannous. That power never fails. It ebbs, but rises again, fresh and inexhaustible. The Eastern walks amid the forms of force of which we talk so glibly, and feels God. In the sun and the wind, in the river's ceaseless flow and the waving of the forest's tops, he is sensible of an awful yet gracious Presence. He hears whispers, and catches the light of glorious garments trailing by. As in Macdonald's charming story, he is ever surprising the gods at play. Those who have listened to Babu Mozoomdar must have felt a singularly sweet devoutness breathing through the rich eloquence of the speaker. Without pre-arrangement, as though it were to him the natural conclusion of his talk with man, he is wont to finish his address with a simple, child-like prayer to 'Our Father who art in heaven'. At family prayer, in my house one morning, sitting after the custom of his people, in his chair, he talked to God in such a way as hushed our hearts into a new feeling of the Presence of Him in whom we live and move and have our being. There were no petitions, but an exhalation, so to speak, of his consciousness of the All-Father, an aroma in the spiritual atmosphere, as when the morning sun draws from the flowers of the field the fresh fragrance in which their life streams up toward its source. I realised then what I had been told of him: 'He lives in God.' The words of Chunder Sen concerning the Hindu gift of yoga, the faculty of apprehending and communing with the Divine Presence came to my mind; and I perceived how truly there was active in this race a spiritual sense which seems numbed and dormant in our Western peoples. That evening I turned, as he had asked me to do, to the Upanishads, 'where,' said he, 'breathes the early and deep Hindu consciousness of God' - and I knew afresh what a revelation there may be to us, who have so much religion and so little living sense of God. As the Hindu spirit breathes in our spirits, we, too, shall find quickening in us this blessed sense of God. So was I brought to 'the gate that looketh toward the East,' and I beheld 'the glory of the God of Israel coming from the way of the East.'

III

The East will help us, through its insistent idealism and its deep abiding sense of God, to a freshened feeling of the true nature of man. As with Nature so with man, our Western thought tends to play upon the surface of the problem. We are intensely busy with our studies of man's nature, and are learning wonderful things about his organisation, truths full of value to the race, for the lack of which the world has lain so long in sickness of body and in superstition of mind. We are coming to know the elements out of which we are composed, the laws of their combination, and the methods of the working of the mysterious forces which fashion us. The human anatomy is laid bare to our eyes, and the wonders of physiology are coming out into the light. The puzzle of the convolutions of gray tissue which make the brain of man is fascinating our wise men, and they cherish swelling hopes of yet guessing the secret of the relations of mind to matter. We have traced so far the broken links of the story of the coming into being of the human race that we have already titled the future history of man, one day to be written, and announced duly to the world the forthcoming book of Genesis. We have analysed the moral nature of man and resolved it into its several elements. We have shown how our ideals of goodness have slowly formed through man's social necessities and clothed themselves with impressive sanctions, until at length they stand so awfully sacred in the inner shrine of the soul, that we bow before them in worship. And having done all this invaluable work, we think that we have solved the problem of man; so that he can be expressed in a chemical formula and labelled in the Museum of Natural History. Having done all which, the East smiles in acquiescence, her eye, as in a vision, fixed upon a 'somewhat' within this chemical compound, and whispers: 'And God (the Eternal) formed man out of the dust of the ground, and breathed into his nostrils the breath of life; and man became a living soul.' That which we miss in the focus of our microscopes, which casts no weight in our balances and slips away in the fires of our crucibles, the Eastern discerns, even as he sees through Nature to its substance, and he knows that man is, in essence - spirit, mind. He will quite humbly receive our Western knowledge concerning the physical constitution and the historic development of man, but then he will return to us that deeper wisdom which reveals the inner and essential being of man. Our crude fancies about an automaton-man will disappear, in the acute sense quickened within us of that spiritual being which is free to will and responsible for its action, as becometh the child made in the image of the Eternal Spirit, the Father of our human spirits. There will come to us the true significance and the deep reality of that ancient belief that in the human spirit speaketh the Divine Spirit; that, as our Hindu-American seer tells us, we are 'always spoken to from behind'; that truth is, as the ancient Hebrew said, the voice of God. Inspiration will then be no theory of the scholar, but the consciousness of the faithful soul. So again we find that 'the glory of the Lord' cometh by the way of the gate whose prospect is toward the East.

IV

The East will help us to a better view of Christ. Whatever the object of the vision, the image of it on the human retina will be largely determined by the nature and condition of the retina itself. Christianity has seen Christ, not as he really was, but as he had appeared to its eyes. Our Western eyes have seen him westernised, distorted in the lenses of Grecian speculation, of Roman institutionalism, of Medieval scholasticism. To German and Scotchman, and Englishman and American, he necessarily shapes himself as best as possible upon their natures.

How grievously the image of Jesus has suffered in this transference, scholars know right well. The image of Jesus which the Christian Church has framed in its theologies is far from a counterpart of the original and real Jesus, so far, that, were most Christians carried back into the age when He was upon earth, and set down in His own Galilee, He might pass them, never known or recognised. How can we ever get back to that far off age and see Him as He was? Simply by getting over into the position of those who today reproduce the life and spirit of His day. In the East, time is not. Today is as yesterday, and our century as eighteen centuries earlier. As the East now reads Him, coming to Him in a free and natural manner - that we may be sure is the nearest approach which we can get to a true image of Him. For Jesus was an Oriental, and only by the Orientals can He be interpreted. A foretaste of what is before us in this recovered view of Jesus we have already, in that touching book of our Hindu preacher, *The Oriental Christ*. At every touch of the Eastern hand the familiar incidents take on fresh lights, and the story stands forth in a new and vivid realism. Renan told us, years ago, that in Judea the story of Jesus became strangely real, and, writing in the East, his book became, with all its faults a revelation of the actual man who walked the land of Galilee eighteen centuries ago. We shall gain a new sense of the veritable actuality of the Man of Nazareth, and we shall never doubt that He was an historic personality. We shall form, as by a new sense opened in us, a perception of what was really the meaning of the words of Him who spake as never man spake. Luther, disputing with Zwingle, his finger on the text - 'This is my body' - closing thus every appeal of the reason against the dogma of transubstantiation, will no longer be possible, when the East reads for us those words. The poetic utterance of the consciousness of the man who felt Himself so completely one with the Father that His own consciousness was, as it were, the consciousness of God, will cease to be hard prosaic proposition for the metaphysic of the schoolmen, and will become the plastic, palpitating words of the Eastern Mystic whose thoughts are feelings, and whose words must therefore needs be poems. When the Oriental comes to them he knows what was meant by them, and we must learn of him. We may thus lose the form which we thought was our Christ - though without the Eastern touch that is fading fast enough from our eyes - but we shall gain a figure which we shall know to be the true Christ. And that will be an image sweet and gracious, holy and, in the deepest sense, divine, before which, in new passion of reasonable reverence, we shall bow most worshipfully, and from whose touch our lives shall flame anew in sacred passion of most loyal love.

One cannot read *The Oriental Christ* without a fresh sense of Jesus and of His good spell upon the soul.

Thus I believe, Jesus will come again to us of the Western World, and we shall all follow Him with new abandonment of love. Let us each ask, as this Hindu asked: 'Not that I might speculate about Jesus but that I might learn to do as He bids me.' Thus as we stand in 'the gate that looketh forward the East' the 'glory of the Lord' cometh 'from the way of the East'.

V

The East will help us in many ways to better general conditions for the religious life. Our occupation amid external activities keeps us aloof from the deep inner life of the spirit. The multiplicity of outward affairs distracts our minds and exhausts our energies. We are too hurried to 'wait upon the Lord'. God may be in the wayside bush speaking to us, but what can we hear as we thunder past in the 'Lightning Express'? How shall we catch the low whispers of the still, small voice, amid the babel of tongues of the Exchange? How, in our chronic tire, shall we climb the heights of contemplation, where our tryst is appointed with the Eternal? We need somewhat of the peace and quiet of those calm Easterns, who have time to pray and leisure to think, and who know the way within the innermost recesses of the soul, where is the Holy Place of God.

We are oppressed with the multitudinous miseries of earth, the wretchedness and woe of this weary world, and we turn the forces of our religious life out upon the work of bettering society. We cannot do otherwise in our Western world, to which Providence has given the powers for the righting of these disorders. The establishment of the divine order in human society, the creation of the proper social conditions for the kingdom of God, is of co-equal importance with the inspiration of the inner personal life. But our ideals suffer in this constraint of work that is upon us. Philanthropy and piety would together form a heavenly pattern for our aspirations. But philanthropy without piety, philanthropy as a substitute for inward experience, for the life hid in God - this can but fashion a maimed and mutilated image. We measure men by their charities, not by their holiness, and find the notes of the true church in the number of their benevolent societies, rather than in the saintly beauty of the lives which they nourish. We condone the faults of him who subscribes freely to our schemes of reform. We gauge the river of life proceeding from beneath the throne of God by the power which it supplies to our mills of reform, and value it because of the wheels it turns. Thus doing comes to dispense with being. We think Christ came to found a society for the organisation of soup kitchens and hospitals. Ah! we greatly need the spirit of those childlike peoples, who stand confused amid the whirl of our vast social mechanism, valuing somewhat lightly our great charities and our brilliant reforms, and dreaming that the kingdom of God is to come without observation; that outward institutions and laws are to crystallise upon a society breathing the spirit of brotherliness and love; that the world is to be lifted into righteousness under the spell of lives all luminously good, and saved from sin by the touch of men in whom is felt the living God. Our Western races are called to the development of earth's resources, and, under the ancient command, to master the earth and 'have dominion over it'. Thus, as we see, is the wealth produced in the division of which all may ultimately share, and the storehouses filled from which the poorest may draw in the time of need. Only thus is society so far advanced already beyond the civilisation of the East that the famines, which there sweep off human beings like flies at the touch of frost, are impossible in Christendom. But in thus being 'not slothful in business' we find it hard to be 'serving the Lord'; and before we are aware of it we find our devotedness to business has become a real devotion, a worship of the Power once known as Mammon, whose altars are in our homes and our exchanges, and on which we offer - ourselves. As every careful, honest student of society sees and tells us, our real religion is a worship of wealth; from which fearful apostasy our wise men see not well how to rescue us; but from which infidelity we would soon be delivered if the higher Eastern spirit breathed upon us its simplicity, its indifference to material possessions, its disregard of riches and the goods that they can buy, its respect for poverty, its sublime upliftedness above the hunger that eats the heart out of our life, its ideals which seem to us as those of some other world, where the question 'What is he worth?' cannot be answered by inspecting a man's bankbook, or opening his coupon-box in the Safe Deposit. The political economy which expresses our ideals of civilisation finds it hard to fit into its order that Son of Man who had 'not where to lay His head'. His ideals it finds unreasonable; His aspirations wild, quixotic dreams. We are told that it is impossible to live a Christian life, that to pattern our lives upon the Master's story would be to undo Society. And thus, our finest impulses and our most generous aspirations, we are taught to smother; and our received theories rally to the aid of our native selfishness, until the language of our Communion Consecration becomes a bitter mockery, which I am sure the disciples of Christ often shrink from repeating - 'And here we offer and present unto

Thee O Lord, ourselves, our souls and bodies, to be a reasonable, holy, and living sacrifice unto Thee.' An Order of 'The Consecrated' as been formed in the Brahmo Samâj; an order whose members, continuing in their daily vocations, consecrate most of their gains to God. As we Christians hear of Hindus doing this, we may well look around us in the Christian Church, to see where are 'the consecrated' among us who follow the Christ.

Oh! for one generation of the climate of the soul in which were born all the great enthusiasms of self-consecration; the contempt of the world which filled the desert with anchorites and the monasteries with men vowed to poverty; the hunger for sacrifice which inspired a buddha, and the greater than a Buddha - Jesus Christ, our Lord. We could safely trust our Western world to set bounds of moderation to this passion of devotion, to keep the altar on which these heavenly fires were lighted from burning up. But oh! for the flame coming down from heaven upon our altars!

Franz Hartmann

Franz Hartmann was a German medical doctor, theosophist, occultist, geomancer, astrologer, and author. He was born on 22 November 1838 in Donauwörth, Bavaria.

Hartmann was an associate of the Theosophical Society's founder, H. P. Blavatsky, and was Chairman of the Board of Control of the Theosophical Society in Adyar, India. In 1896, he founded a German Theosophical Society.

He published the theosophical journals *Lotusblüten* (Lotus Flowers) from 1893 to 1900 and *Neue Lotusblüten* (New Lotus Flowers) from 1908 to 1913. His articles on yoga popularised the subject within Germany.

Described as 'one of the most important theosophical writers of his time', his works include several books on esoteric studies as well as biographies of the German philosopher, Jakob Böhme and the Swiss physician and alchemist, Paracelsus. He translated the Bhagavad Gita into German.

He was one of the original founders of the magical order that would later be known as the Ordo Templi Orientis, together with the occultist,

Theodor Reuss and the mystic, Carl Kellner.

Hartmann's publications include *The Principles of Astrological Geomancy* (1889), *Magic: White and Black* (1886) and *Occult Science in Medicine* (1893).

Franz Hartmann died on 7 August 1912 in Kempten im Allgäu, Bavaria.

Yoga Practice in the
Roman Catholic Church
Franz Hartmann (1911)

The study of comparative religion being one of the objects of the Theosophical Society, it may be of some interest to compare the yoga practices of the Roman Catholic Church with those described in the Oriental writings. We will then find that they are to a certain extent identical, consisting principally in meditation (prayer), shakti, self-control, abnegation, faith, concentration, contemplation, etc, or what Shankarâchârya describes as Shâma, Dama, Uparati, Titíksha, Shraddhâ and Samâdhâna, not to forget bodily posture and the regulation of breath (Prânayâma).

The most detailed instructions are contained in the writings of Ignatius de Loyola, a Catholic Saint, and founder of the (later on ill-reputed) Order of Jesuits. He was an officer in the Spanish army, born the son of a nobleman in the province of Guipúzcoa in the Basque Country in 1491. After having been severely wounded in battle, his mind took a religious turn; he abandoned his military career, became an ascetic, made a pilgrimage to Jerusalem, studied afterwards at Salamanca and Paris, and became in 1541 General of the Order of Jesuits. His writings have been translated into

German by B. Kohler, and the following pages contain some extracts from the same.

The exercises prescribed by Loyola are calculated to develop the powers of the soul, especially imagination and will. The disciple has to concentrate his mind upon the accounts given in the Bible of the birth, suffering and death of Jesus of Nazareth, as if these were actual historical facts. He thus regards them, as it were, as a mental spectator, but by gradually working upon his imagination he becomes, so to say, a participator of it; his feelings and emotions are raised up to a state of higher vibrations; he becomes himself the actor in the play, experiences himself the joys and sufferings of Christ, as if he were the Christ Himself; and this identification with the Object of his imagination may be carried on to such an extent that even stigmata, or bleeding wounds corresponding to those on the body of the crucified Christ, will appear on his body. In this way compassion and love are awakened and developed within the soul, and as the love of a divine ideal is something quite independent of the correctness of the scientific opinion which we may have concerning the actual existence of that ideal itself, this way of awakening divine love by the power of imagination may be very well suited for those for whom love without an object is at first unattainable. Therefore the spiritual exercises of Loyola consist principally of regularly prescribed and gradually ordered meditations and contemplations of the passion of Christ. If properly executed, they may produce freedom from the illusion of self and awaken the power of discrimination (Viveka) between the eternal ego and the temporal self.

The exercises and penances which Loyola taught to his disciples he practiced himself, and they were by no means easy. He spent seven hours in prayer, and scourged himself three times every night for the purpose of subduing the desires of his flesh. Some of the Catholic Orders still practice such severe exercises. The Trappists, for instance, have to work very hard, and their only recreation is prayer. Each brother receives at his entrance to the Order a gown as his only garment, which he has to wear until the hour of his death, without ever being permitted to take it off, whether in daytime or at night, unless it should become so dilapidated as to have to be replaced by a more solid one. Their Matins begin at midnight, lasting for one hour, and one being followed at short intervals by others, so as to allow very little time for rest. They are exposed to the summer heat and have to do without fire in winter, being permitted only a hard bed to sleep on and barely sufficient cover. Moreover they are not permitted to speak with each other or with anybody, and the food they receive is hardly sufficient to keep up their strength.

The Catholic Church, as a whole, may be regarded an as exoteric school of religion, and the different Orders therein as esoteric schools for practising yoga. How far some of these Orders have become degraded and have lost the right to be called schools for yoga, is not our purpose to investigate at present. Certain, however, it is that the Mysteries contained in the Catholic Church are far too high to be grasped by everybody, be he priest or layman, and that the greatest danger which threatens the Catholic Church is the great number of its followers who are incapable of understanding its true spirit, in consequence of which its doctrines are misrepresented and misunderstood.

Nevertheless, in some of the Orders practicing the above-described austerities, some of these Mysteries are still alive. These people lead a life of great hardship, and there are probably only few among our parlour yogis and would-be magicians willing to exchange places with them; but we meet smiling faces and joyous hearts among them, and the fact of their having voluntarily taken upon themselves the Cross of Christ testifies to their intrepidity and sincerity.

Loyola objects to theoretical explanations regarding the divine Mysteries, as they would only gratify scientific curiosity in unripe minds and disturb them; he only gives instructions concerning the practice of meditation etc because, if this practice is properly carried on, the Mysteries will reveal themselves in the natural course of time.

The states of mind under consideration are in their progressive order as follows :

1. *Cogitation.* The state in which the mind is moved and swayed by influences coming from without. These emotions have to be subdued.

2. *Concentration.* The ego assumes power over the thinking process, regulates his thoughts

according to his will, and uses them accordingly.

3. *Meditation.* The ego closely examines the object upon which his mind is concentrated.

4. *Contemplation.* The mind enters the object of its meditation; it becomes an indweller of its sphere.

5. *Sanctification.* The mind becomes pervaded and sanctified by this association with the holy object; it becomes penetrated by its divine influence.

6. *Unification.* The contemplating mind becomes one with the object of its contemplation. To this may be added:

7. *Mortification* or the entire disappearance of the illusion of separateness; there is no separate self which knows, because the knower, the known and the knowledge are one.

The object of meditation is, as has already been stated, the life and suffering of Christ. This is divided into different periods for contemplation, from the Incarnation to the Crucifixion and Resurrection. At first only the memory is called into action by studying the supposed historical facts; next comes the imagination, associating itself with the actors in the divine play, and finally the mind becomes the actor itself; i.e. Christ is born, lives, becomes crucified and resurrected within ourselves. There are numerous instructions given as to how these practical exercises are to be carried out, of which we will mention the following:

The first thing is to free oneself from all sinful thoughts and sensual emotions, and to seek to realise the direct action of the divine will; one should not seek to pry with one's intellect into the divine Mysteries, but wait in humility for their interior revelation. This is far more useful in the end than lengthy explanations on the part of the teacher.

The disciple should, while engaged with one object of meditation during one week, not be informed of what will be the object given to him for the next period; but he should be warned against the aggressions of evil spirits, and have their nature explained to him.

He should meditate for five hours every day, beginning at midnight, each meditation lasting at least one hour, and he must not let his mind wander from the object of his meditation.

He should never make a solemn promise or vow until he is perfectly certain that he is able to keep it; that is to say, until God (the Master) Himself reveals to the soul His readiness to receive her. Then he does not follow his own selfish desires, but obeys the divine will.

The teacher should not seek to pry into the sins and innermost thoughts of the disciple; nevertheless he should observe him, so as to be able to give him such guidance and instruction as his case may require.

Ignorant and uneducated persons cannot be guided in the same manner as those who have more intelligence. No one should be offered spiritual truths which he is not yet ripe enough to grasp or comprehend.

Each meditation should begin with prescribed prayers (The Lord's Prayer, Ave Maria, etc).

The candidate should go to confession once in every week, and take every fourteen days the holy sacrament of communion.

He should separate himself from all his friends and acquaintances, and avoid all external disturbances, directing his mind solely to the service of God. The more he frees himself from all external attractions, the more will he become ready to receive the light, the grace, and the blessing of God.

The disciple should be instructed, according to the degree of his capacity to understand, about the origin and the real object of his life, which is to praise God and to serve Him. He ought to be made to see the relative worthlessness of all earthly things, and the value of that which is of eternal duration.

He should examine himself carefully every day, and compare the results of each examination with those of the previous one, in the same way as a father watches his child to see what progress it makes.

He should carefully avoid all doubt and despair and also all spiritual pride, and not dwell upon his own personal merits, but sacrifice them to God.

Special Directions

Upon rising in the morning the disciple should at once firmly resolve to avoid all those sins of which he wishes to purify himself, and hold fast to that resolution during the day. Before retiring to rest he should examine himself again, to see whether he has been steadfast in his purpose, and it is useful to note his failures in some diary.

Resist and suppress every evil thought as soon as it arises. Avoid all useless talk and gossip.

Look upon all worldly possessions with contempt; desire nothing for yourself, neither bodily comfort nor mental consolation, neither riches nor fame.

The disciple should be indifferent to wealth or poverty, honor or disgrace, suffering and death, and always be ready joyfully to accept martyrdom for the glorification of Christ.

Here follow certain rules which may be found somewhat objectionable from our point of view, namely:

He should never think of agreeable things, such as the joys of Paradise, but always have his mind dwelling upon grief and repentance for his sins, and think of death and the Last Judgment.

He should always keep his room dark and exclude all light, keeping doors and windows closed, except while he is praying, reading or eating.

He ought never to laugh, nor say aught that may cause hilarity in others. He ought never to look at anyone, except at receiving and taking leave of a visitor.

He ought to avoid in eating or sleeping not only that which is superfluous, but even as much as possible of what is considered necessary.

He ought to castigate and lacerate his body by means of lashes, applied with rods or ropes or in other ways, but without injuring the bones. This is for the purpose of doing penance for past sins and for conquering the lusts of the flesh, and also for entering into sympathy with the tortures suffered by our Lord Jesus Christ. (It is hardly necessary to remark that these ascetic exercises have fallen generally out of use, and are only practiced by certain religious Orders at certain times, or by some especially fanatical persons.)

The Three Methods of Prayer

The first method or step is to meditate successfully upon the seven mortal sins, the three powers of the soul, and the five senses of the body. This may be done while standing, sitting, kneeling, or in a recumbent position. While meditating upon the seven deadly sins, compare them with the seven cardinal virtues.

The second step is to meditate about the

meaning of each separate word of the prayer, sitting or kneeling, and keeping the eyes either closed or gazing steadfastly upon some selected spot, and not letting his thoughts or eyes wander around. (Compare Bhagavad Gita VI, 13)

Thus he ought to remain for one hour or more, always beginning his meditation with an invocation, and ending with repeating The Lord's Prayer, Credo, Anima-Christi and Salve Regina. He ought not to proceed to meditate about another word before he has found in the previous one full satisfaction.

The third method consists in regulating the breath according to a certain measure of time. While drawing each breath some word of the prayer ought to be spoken within the heart, so that between each inhalation and exhalation, and during the whole time that this lasts, only one word is inwardly spoken. For instance, if you meditate about the Lord's Prayer, beginning with 'Our Father, which art in heaven,' let your whole attention be directed only to the word our and its meaning, and then proceed to the next word etc.

The Mysteries of the Life
of Our Lord Jesus Christ

These Mysteries cannot be satisfactorily explained to the human intellect; but they can be spiritually grasped by identifying oneself with the events historically described in the New Testament, and mentally participating therein.

In this way the imagination acts upon the will and the emotional nature, causing the higher vibrations of the soul to enter into action, to lift the mind up to the region of spiritual perception, and the love of God to enter the heart. It is then necessary to learn to discern between good and evil influence. Only God has the power to illuminate the mind without any preceding cause; but if there is such a cause, the good angels, as well as the evil ones, may send comfort to the soul; the first ones with good intentions, the evil ones with an evil object (such as to incite vanity or spiritual pride etc) in view, and the evil spirit may assume the shape of a messenger of light for the purpose of leading us to perdition. We therefore ought to examine the origin, current, and object of our thoughts. If the beginning, the middle and the end are good and the object the highest, it is the sign of a good influence; but if the thoughts are disturbed by doubts and turned to inferior objects, it is a sign that an evil spirit is at their back. Moreover the touch of a good influence is mild and sweet, and that of an evil one at first harsh and disturbing; but if the heart is inclined to evil, the evil spirit also enters silently, as if it were into his own house through the open door.

Finally it may be of some interest to hear what Loyola says in regard to the Church:

We must never use any judgment of our own, but be always ready to obey in all things the orders of the true bride of Christ, our holy mother, the Church.

If I see that a thing is white and the Church calls it black, I have to believe in its being black.

We must always approve of and praise the sayings and doings and manners of our superiors, whatever they may be; even if they are not such as can be praised publicly, because to do so would lower these persons in the estimation of the crowd.

One ought not, to the ignorant, to say much about predestination (Karma); because, instead of working for their own improvement, they will become lazy and say: 'Why should I trouble myself? - If it is my predestination to be saved, I will be all right, and if I am predestined to be damned, I cannot prevent my damnation.' One ought also not to speak about the divine grace of God as if it were a gift, rendering all our own works unnecessary. The highest truths are frequently misunderstood, and the best medicine becomes a poison if misapplied.

Some of the rules given by St. Ignatius de Loyola may be objectionable, but nowhere do we find among them the often quoted Jesuitical maxim that the object sanctifies the means. Moreover there is no doubt that while an object, be it holy or unholy, cannot sanctify its means, a holy purpose can and will sanctify the means, provided they are neither holy nor unholy, but indifferent. Thus for instance, the using of a knife upon a man's body may be a holy or unholy act. If it is done for the purpose of cutting his throat, it is unholy; but if the surgeon uses it for saving a person's life it is holy, and the purpose sanctifies the means.

The Roman Catholic Church has originally derived its doctrines and practices, and even its ceremonies, from the Northern Buddhistic School.

Loyola is a true representative of its spirit. His spiritual exercises are in many ways identical with the instructions given in the East for the practice of Raja-Yoga, and a comparison of the two systems may be useful for those who do not merely desire to gratify their curiosity in regard to the astral plane, but desire to become more spiritual by letting the divine powers within their soul become awakened and developed through the influence of divine Love, divine Wisdom, and eternal Life.